D0934599

The Shocking Stories Behind Lightning in a Bottle
and Other Idioms

by Arnold Ringstad • illustrated by Dan McGeehan

Published by The Child's World®
1980 Lookout Drive • Mankato, MN 56003-1705
800-599-READ • www.childsworld.com

Acknowledgments
The Child's World®: Mary Berendes, Publishing Director
The Design Lab: Design and production
Red Line Editorial: Editorial direction

Design elements: Kirsty Pargeter/iStockphoto

ISBN 9781614732365
LCCN 2012932809

Printed in the United States of America
Mankato, MN
July 2012
PA02118

Contents

Bigger fish to fry, 4

Acid test, 5

To keep someone in stitches, 6

Talk turkey, 7

Rain on someone's parade, 8

Mad as a hatter, 9

One-trick pony, 10

Mind your Ps and Qs, 11

All thumbs, 12

Wild goose chase, 13

The bee's knees, 14

Plead the fifth, 15

Crossing the Rubicon, 16

Brownie points, 17

Catching lightning in a bottle, 18

Come out of left field, 19

The whole nine yards, 20

Stool pigeon, 21

Ivory tower, 22

Ants in your pants, 23

Tall tale, 24

Caught red-handed, 25

Horse feathers, 26

The Midas touch, 27

Cat got your tongue, 28

Garden variety, 29

Checkered past, 30

Throw the book at someone, 31

About the author and illustrator, 32

BIGGER FISH TO FRY

MEANING: A person who has **bigger fish to fry** has more important things to deal with.

ORIGIN: No one is sure how the phrase was coined. Its oldest known use was in 1660. Other languages have similar idioms. In French, it is said that a person "has many other dogs to whip."

EXAMPLE: Cindy wasn't too worried about her stubbed toe. She had **bigger fish to fry**: a tough math test in the morning.

ACID TEST

MEANING: An **acid test** is a perfectly accurate test of something.

ORIGIN: The phrase comes from a way to check if a piece of metal is really gold. The tester puts a drop of acid on the metal. If it fizzes, the metal is ordinary. If nothing happens, it is real gold.

EXAMPLE: The championship game will be an **acid test** of the hockey team's skills.

TO KEEP SOMEONE IN STITCHES

MEANING: A person who **keeps people in stitches** makes them laugh so much their sides hurt.

ORIGIN: The phrase refers to a sharp pain in the side called a "stitch."

EXAMPLE: Chris, a standup comedian, **kept the crowd in stitches**.

TALK TURKEY

MEANING: Talking turkey is talking in a direct way, often about business matters.

ORIGIN: The real origin is uncertain. One theory holds that it comes from talks between early American settlers and Native Americans about wild turkeys.

EXAMPLE: Katie decided it was time to **talk turkey** with her parents regarding her weekly allowance.

RAIN ON SOMEONE'S PARADE

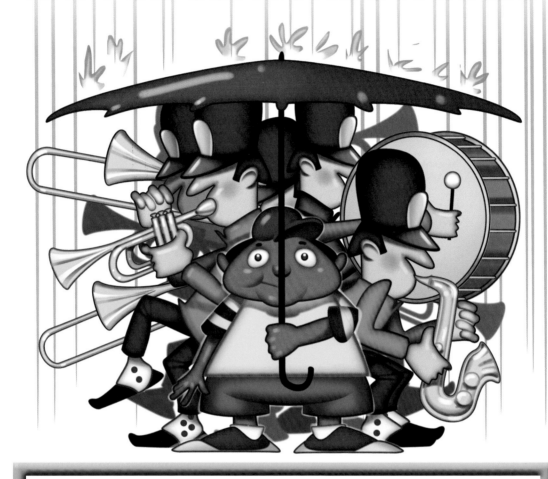

MEANING: To **rain on someone's parade** is to wreck his or her plan or event.

ORIGIN: The phrase came about because parades are cancelled when it rains.

EXAMPLE: Sergio **rained on his friend's parade** when he decided not to rent a bouncy castle for Clark's birthday party.

MAD AS A HATTER

MEANING: A person who is **mad as a hatter** is silly or crazy.

ORIGIN: An old-fashioned method of making hats used the element mercury. People who made the hats were called hatters. Contact with mercury gave the hatters mental and physical problems.

EXAMPLE: Jill's mom danced around the kitchen, acting **mad as a hatter**.

ONE-TRICK PONY

MEANING: A **one-trick pony** is a person or thing that is good at only one thing.

ORIGIN: Experts are unsure of the real origin. Some think it may have come from small traveling circuses from the late 1800s and early 1900s called "dog and pony shows." A bad show might have a pony that could only do one trick.

EXAMPLE: Susanne was good at being funny, but she wasn't good at being serious. As an actress, she was a **one-trick pony**.

MIND YOUR Ps AND Qs

MEANING: **Minding your Ps and Qs** means to be careful or to behave well.

ORIGIN: There are many theories about the origin of this phrase. It might refer to early printing presses. Workers had to set letters individually to use these presses. It was easy to mix up the lowercase "p" and "q" tiles, so workers had to pay close attention.

EXAMPLE: Walt told his friend Bryan to **mind his Ps and Qs** while working at their lemonade stand.

ALL THUMBS

MEANING: A person who is **all thumbs** is clumsy with his or her hands.

ORIGIN: This comes from a phrase from the 1500s: "each finger is a thumb." It became "all thumbs" in the 1800s. It refers to how it would be difficult to use one's hands if all one had were thumbs.

EXAMPLE: Sarah dropped her tennis racquet for the third time this match. She really was **all thumbs** today.

WILD GOOSE CHASE

MEANING: A **wild goose chase** is a hopeless or impossible task.

ORIGIN: The phrase comes from William Shakespeare's play *Romeo and Juliet*. At that time, it referred to a kind of race in which a group of horses followed one lead horse. Their formation looked like a flock of geese. More recently, it refers to the difficulty of catching a wild goose.

EXAMPLE: Christina's search for the rare book was becoming a **wild goose chase**.

THE BEE'S KNEES

MEANING: Something that is **the bee's knees** is excellent.

ORIGIN: This is one of many animal-related catchphrases that came from US popular culture in the 1920s. Similar ones include "the cat's meow" and "the tiger's spots."

EXAMPLE: Calvin thought Grace's new dress was **the bee's knees**.

PLEAD THE FIFTH

MEANING: A person **pleads the fifth** when he or she won't answer a question to avoid getting in trouble.

ORIGIN: The phrase comes from the Fifth Amendment to the US Constitution, one of the founding documents of the United States of America. Part of the Fifth Amendment says that a person can't be forced to testify against herself or himself in a trial.

EXAMPLE: Harold **pleaded the fifth** rather than admit he cheated on the test. He wouldn't answer any of his teacher's questions.

CROSSING THE RUBICON

MEANING: When a person **crosses the Rubicon**, they are going past a point of no return or doing something they won't be able to undo.

ORIGIN: The Rubicon is a river outside Rome, Italy. In ancient Roman times, military leaders could not cross the river with their armies or they would be guilty of treason. The general Caesar crossed the Rubicon with his forces when he wanted to overthrow the government.

EXAMPLE: Dexter **crossed the Rubicon** when he decided to read the 1,200-page novel *War and Peace* for extra credit.

BROWNIE POINTS

MEANING: Earning **brownie points** is receiving credit for completing a small task.

ORIGIN: The exact origin of this phrase is unknown. One popular theory involves the junior branch of the Girl Scouts, known as Brownies. Brownies earn points toward merit badges for doing good deeds.

EXAMPLE: Farouk figured he could earn some **brownie points** by doing the dishes for his mother.

CATCHING LIGHTNING IN A BOTTLE

MEANING: Something that is similar to **catching lightning in a bottle** is difficult or impossible to do.

ORIGIN: The phrase appears to have been coined by a baseball player in the 1940s. It is often used in sports to describe a win against difficult odds. It may have been inspired by the electrical experiments of Benjamin Franklin.

EXAMPLE: John knew that writing a successful book would be like **catching lightning in a bottle**.

COME OUT OF LEFT FIELD

MEANING: A problem that **comes out of left field** is surprising or unexpected.

ORIGIN: The origin isn't known for certain, but it has a connection to baseball. When a player runs around third base toward home plate, he or she turns his or her back to left field. When the outfielder in left field throws the ball to the infield, the runner can't see it coming.

EXAMPLE: Jackie was shocked when her teacher moved the test date up by a week. This had really **come out of left field**.

THE WHOLE NINE YARDS

MEANING: To go **the whole nine yards** is to complete the whole thing.

ORIGIN: The origin of this phrase is unknown, though there are many theories. It might refer to American football, shipyards, the length of ammunition belts on World War II airplane guns, or the volume of cement trucks.

EXAMPLE: Jesse finished every one of his chores in one Saturday afternoon. He really went **the whole nine yards**.

STOOL PIGEON

MEANING: A **stool pigeon** is police informer, someone who gives inside information on criminal activities to the police.

ORIGIN: The word *stool* originally referred to a decoy or distraction. The word *pigeon* is slang for a foolish person. Later, the meaning shifted from a decoy to an informant.

EXAMPLE: The **stool pigeon** told the police all about the gangster's secret hideout.

IVORY TOWER

MEANING: If a person is in an **ivory tower**, they are sheltered from everyday life and activities.

ORIGIN: An ivory tower is mentioned in the Bible as a symbol of purity. The first reference meaning a place where one is out of touch with the real world was made in an 1837 poem by a French scholar.

EXAMPLE: Professor Flanagan was totally focused on his research. He didn't care about things happening outside his **ivory tower**.

ANTS IN YOUR PANTS

MEANING: Someone with **ants in his or her pants** is squirming and moving around restlessly.

ORIGIN: A person with actual ants crawling in his or her pants would probably wiggle around trying to get them out. Someone who squirms around restlessly might look the same way.

EXAMPLE: Steven had **ants in his pants**. He couldn't stop fidgeting in the doctor's waiting room.

TALL TALE

MEANING: A **tall tale** is an exaggerated or fantastical story.

ORIGIN: In the 1600s, the word "tall" also meant fancy; by the 1800s, it was used in North America to mean exaggerated or vivid.

EXAMPLE: Jesse knew Jordan was telling a **tall tale** when Jordan said a dragon ate his homework.

CAUGHT RED-HANDED

MEANING: A person who is **caught red-handed** has been caught in the middle of a misdeed.

ORIGIN: The phrase refers to the blood of a victim on a murderer's hands. It dates in this form to the 1700s.

EXAMPLE: Misty's dad **caught her red-handed** trying to sneak a cookie before supper.

HORSE FEATHERS

MEANING: Something that is **horse feathers** is ridiculous. It is usually used as an exclamation.

ORIGIN: The phrase was first used in American comic strips in the 1920s. It most likely refers to the ridiculous idea of a horse having feathers and flying.

EXAMPLE: "**Horse feathers**!" Jeri said. "There's no way you saw a green fire truck!"

THE MIDAS TOUCH

MEANING: A person with **the Midas touch** can make money from anything they do.

ORIGIN: In a Greek myth, everything King Midas touched turned to gold.

EXAMPLE: Frank had **the Midas touch**. Even though it snowed, he still sold 100 ice-cream cones!

CAT GOT YOUR TONGUE

MEANING: If someone asks "**Cat got your tongue**?" they are asking why the other person isn't talking.

ORIGIN: The origin of the phrase is unknown, but it was probably invented by children. Cats are a popular subject of idioms. The first known use of this phrase in print came in 1881.

EXAMPLE: Devon was silent. "What's the matter?" Mike asked. "**Cat got your tongue**?"

GARDEN VARIETY

MEANING: Something that is **garden variety** is common.

ORIGIN: The phrase refers to the ordinary kind of plant found in a garden, rather than a rare or special type.

EXAMPLE: Sisi was sick, but it was just a **garden-variety** cold. She would be better in a few days.

CHECKERED PAST

MEANING: Someone with a **checkered past** has done a mix of good and bad things. The focus of the phrase is usually on the bad.

ORIGIN: The phrase refers to colors in a checked pattern, such as the red and black squares on a checkerboard.

EXAMPLE: The detective had a **checkered past**. He had once gone to jail for stealing magnifying glasses.

THROW THE BOOK AT SOMEONE

MEANING: To **throw the book at someone** is to punish them harshly.

ORIGIN: The phrase refers to a book of laws. If someone is accused of breaking all the laws in the book, a judge might punish the person harshly.

EXAMPLE: Matt forgot to make his bed, take out the garbage, and feed the cat. He knew his mother was going to **throw the book at him**.

About the Author

Arnold Ringstad lives in Minneapolis, where he graduated from the University of Minnesota in 2011. He enjoys reading books about space exploration and playing board games with his girlfriend. Writing about idioms makes him as happy as a clam.

About the Illustrator

Dan McGeehan loves being an illustrator. His art appears in many magazines and children's books. He currently lives in Oklahoma.